# Prophetic Poetry

T0105706

# Prophetic Poetry

## Inspired by the Holy Spirit

PATRICIA JOHNSON

WestBow
PRESS
A DIVISION OF THOMAS NELSON

WestBow Press books may be ordered through booksellers or by contacting:

WestBow Press
A Division of Thomas Nelson
1663 Liberty Drive
Bloomington, IN 47403
www.westbowpress.com
1-(866) 928-1240

ISBN: 978-1-4497-7439-4 (e)
ISBN: 978-1-4497-7438-7 (sc)
ISBN: 978-1-4497-7437-0 (hc)

Library of Congress Control Number: 2012920971

Printed in the United States of America

WestBow Press rev. date: 12/5/2012

# Contents

# Acknowledgements

A special thanks to my friends, Vietta and Melvin Johnson, for their prayers and encouragement; they hung in there with me a long time. And to Lorraine Reed, who was just such a patient friend, always there to listen and to pray with me and for me. Also, I want to thank my long-time friends Lee and Loretta Baum, who were my small group leaders at the time the Lord gave me a little push through Lee, through his prophetic gifting, to get it together, meaning my book. They have been faithful in encouraging me and praying for me since October 2011. Also, I have to thank my friends from Parkview Assembly of God Prayer Group for their faithfulness and prayers. And a great big thank you to Hilary Wilkins and Corey Buckworth, my grandson and Krista Buckworth for helping me finalize my computer work. What a blessing you are to me! I love all of you!

And most of all, to my Lord Jesus, thank you for allowing me to be your vessel to write this poetry. You've given me a book! Each time I needed help, You were just one prayer away. You are amazing!

# How I Received My Prophetic Poetry

One day, my pastor, whom I had worked for at one time as a secretary, asked me to go to a Salvation Army dinner in his place, along with the staff of our church. Of course I did. I'd never understood what the Salvation Army did besides ringing bells at Christmas and, of course, sharing the gospel of Jesus with the lost. But there had to be more, with their uniforms, etc. I was curious.

We had dinner and then the speakers gave their testimonies about their missions work in Russia. I found their missions work to be awesome! Now I understand where they got their name and why they wear uniforms. They, and we, are soldiers for the Lord.

After it was over, we were walking across the parking lot and suddenly I realized something had happened within me. Something spiritual! I didn't have any way of knowing what, but the next morning, when I did my devotions, I began to worship the Lord. I was singing, "In my life, Lord, be glorified." I heard: "I am glorified, I am glorified, in your life, I am glorified!"

This is when I began to receive my poetry from the Lord. It was in 1998. It was as though the Lord would give me a line from His heart and in the next line, He would say to me what was in my heart. In one particular line, He was saying to me, "Send me, Lord, send me, wherever You would have me go." I was so surprised! It had been birthed in my heart to be in missions. Of course, when we think of missions, we think foreign. However, I'm finding my mission field to be wherever I am. I just love sharing Jesus with everyone that the Lord puts into my path, but my special love is for the young people. Much of my poetry is about sharing Jesus with people. It's a real burden sometimes, and of course, it should be all the time, for all of us!

I've been blessed to spend much time with the Lord, sitting at His feet in worship and praise. And this is when I receive this beautiful poetry. Each poem has a different message for you and for me from Him! Some are about worship, some are more prophetic, and some show His love and compassion and, as in one, His sense of humor. But most of them are about sharing Jesus with the lost.

It is my prayer that each poem will bless you in a special way and that you'll experience His beautiful presence as He speaks to your hearts. If you have never been blessed by knowing Jesus as your Lord and Savior, the last page will show you the way! Praise the Lord!

Remember, as you are reading and being blessed, He loves each and every one of us so much that He shed His Blood and died on the Cross at Calvary for all of our sins. He went to Hell for our sins, in our place. But on the third day, hallelujah, He was resurrected from the grave, and now He is seated at the right hand of God the Father Almighty, interceding for of His people always!

Be Blessed!

—Patricia Johnson

# As I Sit at Your Feet

There's nothing so sweet as to sit at Your feet.
There's nothing that I'd rather do than to bless, bless You forever . . .

The Lord said,

"You're so precious and sweet as you sit at My feet.
As you sing to Me, it's your heart that I see.
It's so pure and true, and your love is too.
There's nothing I'd rather do than to bless, bless you forever.
As you sit at My feet, and our hearts do meet,
your praises you sing are like bells that ring.
Keep singing your songs as each day goes along,
and I'll bless, bless you forever."

# My Testimony

In 1979, I underwent serious surgery. As I went through this, I became a born-again Christian. At this time I found that Jesus Christ was so real. He not only came into my life as my personal Savior but also gave me eternal life and many more years of life on this earth. This is the reason for my love for Him, and this poetry is a gift from Him. As I sat writing this poem, I was actually singing to the Lord in praise and worship. As I sang the first few words, the rest began to come to me, an answer from Him.

# The Holy Spirit

In my life, Lord, be glorified; in my life, be gloried!
How awesome is Your love, my Lord;
    how awesome is Your love!

How majestic are Your words, my Lord;
    how majestic are Your words!

How awesome to be gently taken into Your arms, my Lord.
How awesome to sit at Your feet.

How awesome to be Your daughter, Lord,
    and to be held in Your presence, Lord, is oh, so sweet!

It is my prayer, my Lord, to do your perfect will.
It is a blessing, Lord, to sit at your feet, so very still.

Your presence, my Savior, is so tender and so sweet.
    I just want to sit in Your presence, Lord, and listen as our hearts again do meet.

If I should slip into Your presence in Heaven this very night,
    it would be in the greatest place I could be.
In Heaven there's only love and peace and joy,
    and, You, my Lord, would be my Light!

But I can't leave yet, my Jesus;
    I still have a work to do.
There are so many lost people out there, and I have to finish my book of poetry too!

My poetry is a gift from You, my Lord.
It's a treasure, and it has to be completed, that's for sure!

I'm excited, my Lord, to be Your vessel to help win souls.
And my prayer for this book of poetry is
    that souls will be won to Jesus
    and each one will be made whole.

I give You all the Glory, my Lord, for all the work that is being done.
Without You, Holy Spirit, I sure wouldn't be the one!

You see, the devil tried to take my life, my mind, and everything I had.
To miss the Holy Spirit's guidance is never good but will always turn out bad!

So when the Holy Spirit spoke this time, as clearly as a bell,
    I was running for my life, for sure, or I would not be going to Heaven;
    I'd be going to Hell!

Blessed Holy Spirit, You "delivered me from the snare of the fowler, and the
    noisome pestilence." (Psalm 91:3)
You hovered over me and protected me when the devil tried so hard to win.

But You, Holy Spirit, spoke to me very clearly and told me what to do.
I grabbed my clothes and left where I was, and You, Holy Spirit,
    delivered me, and I can't do a thing but praise You!

The devil knows the plans you have for my life—
    souls to save and poems to write.

He also knows what's ahead of me, and he's not happy that you've set me free.
With Your help, Holy Spirit, I'm going forth, serving my Lord Jesus in total victory.

# Now Is the Time

"Now is the time" has been spoken to me,
by a man of God, to only me.

This had been spoken to me a while ago.
When I heard it again, I said, "This is for me, I know."

The risen Savior is coming soon,
and to His Spirit I want to stay in tune.

There's been so much confusion and strife in my life.
I just want happiness and joy and love —to be someone's wife.

I've just taken a job by the leading of the Lord.
I put out so many résumés, to not take this one, I couldn't afford.

Then the word came forth that "now is the time."
This is my job, from the Lord—this is mine!

"Back to the fiery furnace," the Lord said to me.
"But this time, you're going in to set others free."

He said I'd been through the fiery furnace, came out like pure gold.
But this time when I come out, it will be something to behold.

Souls are waiting, watching, and looking, you see.
For the truth! Who is it who will set them free?

So the Lord said tonight on TV, "Now is the time." He said it to me!
I heard it again, my confirmation, my present assignment. Lord, I see!

"Joshua," the pastor said, "had to go into the Promised Land.
He didn't go alone; he went with the Lord, hand in hand."

So it is with me, the Lord said. Many are waiting.
I have work to do, hand in hand with Jesus!
There can be no hesitating!

# Willing to Obey

In my life, Lord, be glorified.

The Lord said,

"Always, always, always, am I glorified in your life.
You will do anything to discourage any kind of strife.

I welcome your praise and your worship from your heart.
As long as we're alone and you read My Word,
  and worship Me in song, My love to you I will impart.

You've been through a lot of trials and tribulations in these recent days.
But you've been crying out, 'Lord, teach me Your ways.'

The trials and tribulations are difficult, it seems.
But remember, I am with you always, and I'll bring you through
  each one with answers to your dreams.

It took courage for you to say, 'Not my will, but yours, Lord, today.'
Your willingness to sacrifice, 'something different,' you would say!
You will find many blessings, because My Spirit you're willing to obey."

# Why Aren't You Praying?

I call to My people, I call them to pray.
I will be coming back for My church, much to many of My people's dismay.

You see, the hour has come when My people must worship Me and worship Me
    each day.
But many are too busy going about their own way.

I want My people to love Me so much that they will put Me above all else.
No more sports or games when I ask. They will worship Me and pray and forget
    about themselves.

There are wars going on in the whole wide world.
There are children starving, little boys and little girls.

Where are My children claiming to be like Me?
Their hearts should be burdened to pray for others; if they'd just look through My
    heart, they could see.

Without prayers from the church of the living God,
the devil will trample on every soldier and every little child.

Be aware, My church, I'm coming back soon.
Be aware, My church, to My Spirit be in tune.

You must be ready to hear My call.
You must be ready, or you will fall.

I love My church; I have waited so long.
I want to bring you all home, and together we'll rejoice with a song.

*Prophetic Poetry*

Don't be foolish and be deceived.
Get down on your knees, seek Me in prayer, and you will see.

The devil seeks to devour all those he can.
But through your prayers, his works will be defeated by the Son of Man.

So take on the burden to pray, pray, pray.
And you'll all be home with Me, much to the devil's dismay.

The Father is hearing the prayers of some,
but He wants to hear the prayers of all the Church, one by one.

# When Storms Come Your Way

In the midst of a storm, I look to my Lord.
To look to anyone else, I just can't afford.

He has healed me and comforted me in a way that only He could.
He loves me, because of His Son, not because I'm someone who's good.

You see, I'm a sinner who's been saved by Grace.
Because of the Blood of Jesus, I can look up to my Lord's beautiful face.

On my knees, with my hands lifted high,
I look up to my Father, crying, "Why, Lord, why?"

I've been through so much, Lord, I can't take much more.
That's when He takes my hand in His and says, "This battle is Mine, not yours."

He reminds me of His Word in Exodus 14:14:
"The Lord shall fight for you, and ye shall hold your peace."

When the storms come, just run to Him, and fall on your knees!

# We Must Stay in Tune

The Lord Jesus Christ is the King of Kings and Lord of Lords.
He is the Alpha and Omega and so much more!

He is the great High Priest of the holy church today.
He is our advocate to the Father and just has to pray and pray.

At this very hour, the enemy of our souls is seeking whom he may devour.
If we don't pray and read the Word, to fight these battles we'll not have the power.

This is why Jesus is praying so hard and so fast.
He's praying that each of His children will have the power and strength to last.

As each day passes, the battles get worse.
That's why we need to read the Bible and know it verse by verse.

The Lord Jesus Christ defeated the devil on the Cross at Calvary.
Through His precious Blood, shed for our sins, we have the victory.

He's our High Priest, our deliverer, the lover of our souls.
He died for each and every one of us, and wants to make us whole.

Just seek His face, and through God's Grace, just know that you'll receive
a healing touch from the Master's Hand, if only you'll believe.

He's coming soon, so stay in tune to the Holy Spirit within.
When the trumpet blows, we all will know we're going home to be with Him!

# A Forgiving Heart

In my heart Lord, be glorified:

The Lord said:
"I am glorified,
I am glorified,
In your heart, I am glorified.

As you sit at My feet, with your singing so sweet,
there's nothing that I'd rather do than to bless, bless you forever.

When you sing those sweet songs
as each day goes along,

with your heart you do sing,
"Lord, in my heart change everything."

Search my heart Lord, if there be any wicked ways.
Make me Your way Lord, is what you do say.

If there be any way that is not pure before You,
change me, oh Lord, it's Your will I long to do.

Purity only comes from a heart that's willing to change.
In molding and shaping, there can be great pain!

It isn't easy to allow Me to increase in you.
But this has been your prayer for many years, 'tis true.

Unforgiveness has been there, and from your heart I've taken it out.
You've said, "Thank you Lord," with a praise and a shout!

*Prophetic Poetry*

Unforgiveness, you see, can harden your heart.
It can cause you to falter and from Me you'll depart.

You have to forgive, as My Word says to you.
Or when you stand before Me in Heaven, I'll have to say,
"I did not know you."

So don't take it lightly, search your heart every day.
"Thank You, Lord, for changing it this day."

When you think you are perfect and see everyone else's sin,
take time to say, "Father, look at me, within."

Be sure that you're right with your Father above.
You're His daughter and He wants you to be filled with His love.

He's your Creator, making you for His pleasure.
Filled with His love is the only way that you will measure.

# All Will Have Heard

Thank You, Lord Jesus, for the Blood that You shed.
"I love you, My children," was written in red.

"The stripes that I bore on My back that day
were to heal your diseases and show you the way.

I love you so much that My heart breaks each day
to think that My children cannot even pray.

There are places in the world where the devil's strongholds are firm.
It won't be much longer 'til he's going to burn.

I'll not let him keep hurting, killing, and robbing Mine.
My children were made for My pleasure—their lights have to shine.

The devil has plans to continue to have his way.
He wants My children, he's made them his prey.

It's not going to happen. Your Heavenly Father has seen so much.
They're My prophets, My anointed. The devil knows he's not to touch.

My wrath is coming quickly, My children must be wise.
They're not praying enough, they're listening to the devil's lies.

They're suppose to be reading and studying My Word,
to be fasting and praying, seeking My face, to be heard.

My children are busy trying to keep their bills paid,
instead of paying their tithes and trusting in Me to make a way.

Whatever happened to Malachi 3:10, 11, & 12?
If they'd go to church on Sundays and pay their tithes,
their bills would be paid and so many more would be made well.

Do they not read in Matthew, chapter 24?
It's warning them of all the signs that they're seeing,
and so much more.

The ten virgins—five were wise and five were not.
When those five, left behind, came to Jesus,
at last prepared and knocked—Jesus said to them, "I know you not!"

It will happen again, it's in My Word.
That's why I have warned you. My Word says, "All will have heard."

# As In the Days of Noah

This is the time that the days are growing long.
Not just to work, or play, or to sing a song.

This is the time to be oh so aware
that the Coming of Jesus is so near.

This is the time that people laugh, mock, and persecute My children,
as they witness and love them and try to warn them.

They think they're crazy, not in their right minds, imagining all these things.
They think they're strange, going to church where they go to sing.

One day real soon, they're going to find My children gone.
Millions of people disappearing, by the Holy Spirit they will be drawn.

This is the beginning of their troubles and woes.
Fear of this kind these people don't really know.

These people, whose hearts are so hardened they could only laugh at
    those that are Mine.
Then they'll look around them and realize they've been left behind.

Disaster will be upon them everywhere they seem to look.
They'll just think and remember what was said to them.
They should have read My Book!

Mockers and scorners full of hatred for Mine.
They'll just remember My children were one of a kind.

They'll run to and fro, looking for shelter, which they'll not find.
They'll ask then for help—they should have listened to Mine!

Kindness? This they will not find.
There will be no one who loves or cares, only hatred, as they hated Mine.

They'll have some decisions to make—accept the Lord Jesus Christ or take
The Mark of the Beast?—Spiritually, they'll suddenly be awake!

These people will suffer so greatly in these days.
Their decisions will be made—hopefully for Christ—He's the only way!

If they do receive Jesus, they'll be sentenced to death.
At this time taking their last breath.

But at that time in Heaven with Jesus they'll be.
And all the born-again believers they will once again see.

But that's what I want for them, to be one with Mine now!
But they're going to learn the hard way, and before Me, they'll all bow.

It's coming so soon people, listen to My children now.
They love you, they care, get saved. My children will show you how.

Remember, children, how Noah built the ark?
The people in those days thought he was crazy as a lark.

Suddenly the rains came down.
The people wanted Noah to let them come on the ark—
they screamed, "Please! Now!"

As it was in the days of Noah, so is it now!

# Ask Me Jesus

Follow Me, and I will make you fishers of men.
—Matthew 4:19

Every time I look at You, My Lord, I see beauty in Your eyes.
I see Your beauty in the little children, and I feel Your love as each one of these
    little ones cry.

I feel the love and compassion in Your heart
when I see those poor and needy people—in their lives You have no part.

I feel Your hurt, dear Lord, each time I see a brother fall.
This makes me realize, dear Lord, how Your heart must ache
when in pain, Your children to You do not call.

When I feel such compassion for others that it brings tears to my eyes,
it is not me, My Lord, but You in me. This to me is no surprise.

Ask me dear Jesus, what You would have me do
to help these hurting people to come to know you.

# To Be Born Again

On this day the Lord has said,
"The day is near when people will have great fear and dread."

To the Father above, the sin on this earth
is greater sorrow than a child's stillborn birth.

The Father in Heaven, who looks upon the sin,
is angered greatly from within.

The Heavenly Father gave us commandments to live by.
But most of the children to whom He gave birth, to live by His commandments,
        most won't even try.

They've heard many people say, "You must be born again."
But to them, it's a joke; they just continue to sin.

They laugh as they curse and even kill.
Some of them laugh at the blood of others they spill.

There are those who live in adultery, a commandment of God that you shall not do.
But they consider it not a problem; it's a way of life, 'tis true.

But the day is coming very soon, you can be sure.
Many will be going to Heaven, but only the holy and pure.

Those who choose to do these other things, even after being warned,
will go to Hell, unless, being born again, their hearts shall be torn.

Jesus died on the cross for their sins, His blood He shed.
He went to Hell for their sins, but praise God, He rose from the dead.

Hallelujah to our Savior, Jesus Christ, our Lord.
To not become born again we cannot afford.

Read it in the Bible, John 3:3.
Look at it yourself, read it and see.

The Lord will not tarry much longer, it's true.
He's calling, He's calling. "Come to me," He's calling to you.

# Christmas Gifts? He's the Best!

Every time I hear my Lord,
His still small voice I listen for.

He blesses me when I hear Him call.
Were I to stand in His presence, I would surely fall.

He has filled me with His Spirit and I must go forth
to let His children know they have to rejoice.

This is the time of which the prophets foretold.
These are the days when the glory of our Lord we shall behold!

The former and the latter rains are falling hard.
My people shall go forth and they shall go far.

The mission of My people is to share the Good News.
They must be bold and courageous; this they must choose!

Time is drawing near for My children to come home.
I want many to come with them, not just them alone.

So My children, hear My voice.
This is My command, not a choice!

Let not the gospel from your hearts depart.
Keep witnessing and sharing your Lord with all your heart.

Let not the season cause your mission to become second, but first.
Remember, this is the season of your Savior's birth.

Share him, share him, share him with great zeal.
And know that the souls that you win to Jesus—Salvation is for real!

Christmas gifts?—He's the best!

# Dwelling In Your Presence

Dwelling in Your presence, Lord, is something to behold.
Dwelling in Your presence, Lord, will make me very bold.

When I'm sitting at Your feet, Lord, that is so very sweet.
I want to say, I love You, Lord, as once again our hearts do meet.

When I'm sitting in Your presence, Lord, listening to Your voice.
My mind is on the anointing Lord; I want to just rejoice!

The anointing of the Holy Spirit is so powerful and real.
I have to concentrate on what You say, Lord, and not on what I feel.

This poetry You've given me is a blessing to me, Lord.
I want to share it with the world and let them feel my joy.

Lord Jesus, I'm Your vessel and I'm open to Your will.
Just fill me with this poetry until it overflows and spills.

# Father, Father

Today my dear Lord, as I was sitting at Your feet,
I was dwelling in the secret place of the Most High, and oh, how sweet!

I welcome Your presence, my dear Jesus, wherever I may be.
Today while sitting at the park, I just closed my eyes and smiled; I did not have to see.

While You and I are all alone, nothing else seems to matter.
As I'm sitting in Your presence, Lord, I don't even mind the children's chatter.

I ask You, dear Lord, to strengthen me and help me to be bolder too.
As I was sitting in the park today, I wanted to tell lost souls about You.

As I was sitting there, being embraced by Your love,
the people all around me didn't even know that You were watching from above.

Father, Father, hear my prayer,
I pray that those people in the park will still be there.

I pray that your anointing for witnessing would really be on me.
And I pray, as I give them the Good News of Jesus,
they will not want to flee.

It is such a blessing, Lord, to be a vessel of Your love.
When I share Jesus with these people, I pray they'll know that You are above.

While I was sitting in the park, dear Lord, You were making me so aware,
of while I was being blessed, dear Jesus, it was You I needed to share!

Thank You, Jesus, for this beautiful day,
and for helping me Jesus, to know how much more I need to pray!

*Prophetic Poetry*

# Giving of Yourself

In my life, Lord, be glorified.

The Lord said:

"I am glorified through those tears of love.
I am Your Lord and Savior; I see You from above.

I watch You every day, as You go to and fro.
And I see a little blessing coming, through someone only I could know.

You see, your prayer has been that you would be a blessing to others.
Today you've not only blessed your children, but you've also blessed
    Your Heavenly Father.

You spend so much of your time, seeking things to give to someone else.
You don't ever have to be concerned about thinking only of yourself.

Today you've not only blessed a man who's known he was dying of cancer.
But today you've given him the hope that perhaps the Lord Jesus is the Answer.

When you've given of yourself to someone who has no hope,
you can be sure there is a special blessing ahead, you're sure not at the end
    of your rope!

The devil doesn't think much of it, but there's nothing he can do.
When your friend gets with His Savior, he'll be healed, and he'll know
    the Bible is true."

# Jesus Did It on the Cross

Jesus, King of Kings, the Prince of Peace, the Mighty God is He.
He's the Living Word, the Great I Am, over all principalities.

Use His Name and the devil's knees shall bow.
If he doesn't obey, show him the Word, and it will show him how.

The devil, he's defeated. Jesus did it on the Cross!
The devil's a liar, a cheat, he's out to rob, but he's got to bite the dust!

It is written, the Bible says, in James 4:7,
"Resist the devil, he must flee," he can't do anything, but listen.

He's a defeated foe. Jesus did it on the Cross!
We're children of God; resist the devil—he has to listen to us.

It's not just us he listens to, it's Jesus living within.
When we speak, because of the anointing, all he hears is, "devil, you just cannot win!"

He tries so hard to bring about fear to those who aren't quite sure
of who they are in the Lord Jesus Christ, but just like Jesus, they are holy and pure.

It is written, we're just like Jesus, "of a royal priesthood," we are.
"I'm raining down on those who need the Holy Ghost and fire."

I want you to see what happens when you resist the snake himself.
The devil flees from the Name of Jesus, but he'd like to hide under a shelf.

He's been defeated by the Lord Jesus Christ, this he already knows.
His time is so short, he's so nervous, he runs on his tippy toes.

He's out to destroy and defeat My children, but knows he just can't win,
especially when he sees what happens when My children worship Me and begin to
    dance and sing.

It's a hallelujah time, it's time for a Jericho March.
The Lord is coming soon, it's already begun in all My children's hearts.

I see the joy, I see the love, I see the hunger and thirst.
It's all so real, it's what you all feel. It's so spontaneous, not time to be rehearsed.

As My coming draws near, the battles will grow, because the devil's counting
    his time.
He'll attack My children, who are so prayed up, he already knows he can't have
    them, they're Mine!

Their strength and courage all comes from Me!
They have My Word, they have each other. They have the victory!

It's through the Blood of the Resurrected Lord Jesus Christ.
The battle's been won, the devil's defeated, he might as well go sit on ice.

I think he should cool himself now, because he sees the Lake of Fire.
When the Lord Jesus Christ comes back again, the devil knows he's made his bed,
    and it's not his heart's desire.

It's going to be hot for a long, long time, and he'll tempt My children to sin.
He wants them in the Lake of Fire to burn along with him.

"Listen, My children, to your Lord Jesus Christ. Read My Word, pray in the spirit,
    fast and seek My Face.

I'll teach you and instruct you in the way you should go.
I'll speak to your hearts, you'll plead the Blood, and together we'll win the race!"

# God's Grace—My Salvation

In my life, Lord, be glorified.
For my sins, Lord, You willingly died.

In my heart, Lord, You've changed me so.
You've molded me and shaped me, as only You could know.

You have given me so much love and happiness, 'tis true.
I just long to be in Your Word, Lord, and so alone with You!

You're my life, my Savior and my Lord!
I just want to know Your love so much more!

You are my deliverer and healer, my redeemer forevermore.
How I ever lived without You, I'm not really sure.

In my life has been so much heartache and disappointment, I was just so disillusioned!
I cried out, "God, what's going to happen to me? I'm either going to die or end up
     in an institution!"

That's when You, my Heavenly Father, began to answer my prayers.
You let me know that You were right there, not "upstairs."

He let me know that my daughter was now His.
I could not understand, but what I saw in her, I wanted this!

She was so peaceful, so mild and oh so sweet!
"Come with me, Mom." Her Lord she wanted me to meet.

I said, "My child, in a cult I hope you've not gotten."
"Oh no, Mom!" she smiled. "On that ground I have not trodden."

So off I went with her one week
to this special church, her Lord to meet.

At the end of the service, after I'd heard The Word,
I knew this was what it was all about, it was My Lord! He's the one I wanted to serve!

I had heard The Word and had listened to all the praise.
And after the service there was so much love, I was just so amazed!

These people, they knew me not.
Their love was so special that my problems I forgot.

I just know that when I cried out to my God,
He was right there to draw me to Him, to know His love.

I have no doubts that my Lord hears my prayers.
He lives in my heart, He's right here with me. I don't think of Him as being upstairs.

We all know that the word "upstairs," is just another word for Heaven.
Unsaved people use this word, they have been filled with so much leaven.

So I pray for their salvation, to know Jesus as their Lord and Savior,
To repent of their sins and ask Him into their hearts. This is such a small favor.

And yes, this is a favor to them,
to pray for their salvation, to see them saved from their sins.

You see, my sister prayed for me one night.
For three hours, she knew she was in a fight!

There was a soul in balance, of this she just knew.
Victory in her family, she was told, 'tis true.

It was me, you see!
Her love and time she spent on her knees helped bring me into God's family.

Now it's my turn to pray and fast and seek His face
for the salvation of others, for them to know His love and His
amazing Grace.

# A Vision I had of the Rapture

> For the Lord Himself will come down from Heaven, with a loud command. With the voice of the archangel and with the trumpet call of God, and the dead in Christ will rise first. After that, we who are still alive and are left, will be caught up together with them in the clouds to meet the Lord in the air. And so we will be with the Lord forever.
>
> —I Thessalonians 4:16-17 (NKJV)

When I was a new Christian, I was listening to a song by Sandy Patti entitled, "We shall behold Him." I had my eyes closed. As I was listening to the words, "and we shall behold Him," I suddenly had a sensation of being lifted up, and I saw other people like me, with their arms down at their sides, going up in the sky as I was. I looked over to my left, and on a white cloud, I saw Jesus kneeling down on one knee, looking over the cloud. Then He looked over to me, with His long brown, curly hair and white robe and He was smiling. It was as though He was saying to me, "Finally, I'm bringing My Church Home!" I shared this with my pastor and he said, "Pat, I can't believe you're saying that. I had the same vision. The only difference was, I yelled over to my wife, "Isn't this wonderful?"

The next poem, "Going Home," is based on this vision.

# Going Home

In the midnight hour, when all was still,
The Lord Jesus came to get His church—it was such a thrill!

The angels sounded their trumpets and the dead in Christ did arise.
Those who did remain were changed and quickly filled the skies.

Jesus, who waited upon a great big cloud,
looked at His church and laughed, oh so loud!

He had waited so long for this very moment to arrive.
The thrill was so great, He could hardly blink His eyes.

He looked at His church arising, one by one.
He looked into their eyes, smiled, and said, "You're coming Home!"

When they arrived in Heaven, the Father welcomed them and said,
"Welcome home, My Children," it was just as I had read.

Awaiting them also was Jesus, their Savior, whom they had longed to see.
They all bowed their heads and quickly fell to their knees!

Their Savior, their Lord, their God, in His presence they finally were.
They'd made it through their trials and tribulations, and now, eternally,
would be with The Living Word.

Jesus, our Savior, who died on the Cross for our sins,
opened His arms so very wide, and to Heaven welcomed us in.

We are so very blessed to be His children, you see.
Without the Blood that Jesus shed, we'd none have life eternally.

We'd finally made it to Heaven with our Lord Jesus Christ,
without batting an eyelash once, not even twice.

# How Deep Is My Love

There's nothing so sweet as to sit at Your feet.
There's nothing that I'd rather do than to be like You, than to be like You!

The Lord said:

Every time I hear My daughter's cry of despair,
I put My arms around her, to let her know I care.

There are so many things that My daughter can never know.
If I allowed her to have the knowledge she seeks,
I'd not have the pleasure to let My child grow.

She feels so unworthy and very alone,
but I've chosen a work for her and on this path she must go.

I've always had My hand on her life,
even as she has suffered great pain and great strife.

I've watched her grow through these things, never alone.
I've carried her through these trials, preparing her to come home.

She's always praying, "Lord, use me this day."
She just doesn't realize how I've guided her in every way.

She begins to pray when she opens her eyes,
and asks me to help her to be ever so wise.

As I watch her each day, going down life's narrow road,
she lets Me help her carry much of her load.

As I look down at her sweet smiling face from above,
I just let her know by My Spirit, how deep is My love.

When she struggles and strains to know that I'm there,
she gets down on her knees, lifts her hands to her Lord, and begins her sweet
    prayer.

She's had so many heartaches and so many trials,
and yet through every one of them she looks up to those around her and continues
    to smile.

I often wonder if she really knows of the depth of My love,
when it's in her heart that I live, not way above.

I have given her many more years to live than she can ever imagine.
When she gets to Heaven, she'll find many rewards without even asking.

There's a pearl here and another pearl there, there's a little box to open, which
    she'll do with great care.

There are so many things that she'll laugh at, with great joy,
But the greatest of all, will be seeing her Savior, Jesus— her Greatest Joy!

# I Love You, My Child

In my life, Lord, be glorified, be glorified.
In my life, Lord, be glorified today.

The Lord said:
I am glorified, I am glorified.
In your life, my child, I am glorified.

It is so sweet when our hearts do meet
as you sing your songs, from your heart to Me.

Each day you pray, "Lord, use me this day.
Help me to be a blessing to someone in a special way."

I want you to know, My child, that you have a way
of lighting up a person's heart with the words that you say.

As you ministered to your new friend today,
giving her scriptures from the Word, this is your way.

You lifted so many burdens that she carried so heavily,
she just praised Me and praised Me, her heart felt so free.

She gave you a Word from Your Lord, which you did not hear.
What she said to you, My child was, "The answers to your prayers are so very near!"

At this time and moment you're willing to serve others for Me
as a volunteer worker in a hospital, being my hands extended,
comforting hurting families.

While comforting and serving to the best of your ability,
your prayers are being answered, while serving others for Me.

Your work may seem a little unusual, but not for where you are.
You're going to meet your new assignment,
the most wonderful person you've ever known by far!

# I Worship You, Lord

I love You, my Lord, with all of my heart.
I love You, my Lord, from You I'll never depart.

I have been so blessed by Your love and gentleness.
I just sit in Your presence and in Your arms I do rest.

Your presence, oh Lord, is so sacred and holy to me.
I just close my eyes and worship You in spirit and in deed.

I have reverence for You, Lord, You are My Father God.
I have reverence for You, Lord, when in Your presence I do trod.

I worship You, my Lord, with all my heart and all my soul.
I thank You, my dear Lord, for making me whole.

Miracles, my Lord? Oh, I have had many!
To worship You, dear Lord, reasons? Oh, I have so many!

I love You, dear Lord, as I sit here at Your feet.
I worship You, dear Lord, as our hearts again do meet.
Your presence, oh Lord, is so precious to me!

Sing:

I worship You with all my heart, there is none like You.
I love You, Lord, with all my heart, that is all I want to do.
I give You praise, for You are my righteousness.
I love You, Lord, with all my heart, there is none like You!

# If They Only Knew Jesus as I Do

This night as I lay my head down to go to sleep,
I was crying out to my Father for my loved ones and all I could do was weep.

I can't take anymore, Father, I don't know what to do.
I just can't make my loved ones get saved, I have to give them to You.

When I see them all going in their own little ways,
I just have to say, "Father, please bring them Your way."

I cry out, "Father, save them! It's your promise to me!"
Touch their hearts and open their eyes that they may see.

Let them know that through the Blood of Jesus, they can be saved.
To know Him as their Savior will give them peace—He's the only way!

One is sick in the body and crying with much pain,
but to ask Jesus to heal him, to him there is no gain.

They have to have faith and believe that Jesus is there
to touch them and heal them and to keep them from despair.

There is no one who will ever do what Jesus has done for me and for you!

He took those stripes upon His back, beaten beyond recognition.
To heal us of all sickness and disease was His provision.

There will never be another chance to receive Him into your hearts
if he decides it is your time from this earth to depart.

# How to Get Saved

So take a good look at your life today
and search your heart for any wicked ways.

If you see there is sin,
just ask forgiveness, open your heart and ask Jesus to come in.

There He is standing at your heart's door today.
"Let Me come in," He is saying.

Just fall on your knees and begin to pray.

# In His Presence

In the presence of the Lord, I am sitting at His feet.
As I worship Him and praise Him, with great love our hearts do meet.

I told the Lord how wonderful it is to be His child.
He held me, oh so tight. In His presence, I could only smile.

It's so awesome, the presence of the Lord!
To miss sitting at His feet is just something I could never afford.

Being in His presence is greater than all the silver and gold.
To have Him tell me He loves me is just something to behold.

I want to share my Jesus with everyone I see.
I want to tell them that His love for them is so very free.

Since I have asked Him into my heart,
I have been given a brand new start.

I never knew what it was to be held in my Father's arms.
Now I feel safe and secure and know to me will come no harm.

He is my peace, my joy, my strength, my everything!
He is the Lord of Lords and the King of Kings.

He's soon to come for His Church, you see,
and when the trumpet blows, into His arms will I flee.

His church is so great and will be greater when He calls,
and when we look into His beautiful eyes,
one by one, on our knees we the Church, will fall,

Home at last, with our Savior and Lord,
in His peace, His presence and His love and His joy.

No more battles and no more fears.
No more rejection and no more tears.

We've fought the good fight of faith, as He asked,
and now we're Home, finally, Home at last!

# In My Name
## You'll Do Many Things

In my life, Lord, be glorified:

Oh child of Mine, so pure and sweet,
without My love, you'd be incomplete.

Your hunger and thirst for things above
lets Me know how true is your love.

Your love for Me is above all things.
Your love for Me causes the angels to sing.

My plan for your life is coming to pass.
It won't be long when you'll say, "Father, it's here at last!"

You've hungered and you've thirsted and you've cried out to Me
to change you and mold you and make you more like Me.

"Make me what you want me to be, Father," I've heard you pray.
Your prayer has been answered, it's coming your way.

In your life, My child, you've had many heartaches.
And in your life, My child, you've made many mistakes.

But you've come to Me with a humble heart.
You've loved Me from the very start.

I've heard you cry out, "Father, forgive me, I've sinned once again."
But that's why I'm your Savior, your Lord, and your friend.

I knew the day would come when you would cry out to Me,
"Please forgive me Jesus, I want to be yours, I want to be free!"

So today, you have begun a brand new journey with your Lord.
Remember your calling, seeking My face always—to do otherwise, you cannot
    afford.

Fasting and praying, being still with your Lord,
Reading your Bible, singing your songs to Me will keep you filled with joy.

Remember, My child, I've chosen you, you haven't chosen Me.
I shed My Precious Blood on the Cross, so that you could be free.

You'll do many things in the name of your Lord,
Jesus, the name above all names, the only name for sure!

# Born Again

Sitting at Your feet, in Your presence so sweet,
   once again, here we are together—our hearts do meet.

In my praise and worship of You, my Lord,
   I feel such peace and joy and blessings so real.
   In Your presence, oh Lord, I want to praise You so much more!

As the Holy Spirit leads me, another song of praise I hear.
   And as I'm singing to You, my sweet Jesus, I'm in Your presence, so precious
   and so dear.

Let me praise You, my dear Jesus, as I never have before,
   and let me sing to You, my Jesus, because You are my Lord.

I love You, my Jesus, as I never thought could be,
   but then I was not born again and therefore could not see.

The songs that I've heard before have never meant a thing,
   but now that I've been born again, in my heart my songs simply seem to ring.

The finer things of life to me once meant material things,
   but since the day I was born again, I just want to sing and sing and sing.

I once was a sinner and my sins I could not see.
   When I received You, Lord Jesus, into my heart,
   my eyes opened and I was set free.

You have saved me from my sins, from Hell and the grave.
   I'm on my way to Heaven, Jesus—You have paved the way.

*Prophetic Poetry*

Jesus is the Lord of my life and the lover of my soul.
He has washed me in His precious Blood, and has healed and made me whole.

## Vision
As I began to sing to the Lord in praise and worship, because I love Him so, I saw in a vision the Lord Jesus sitting at the right hand of the Father and as I began to sing, "I love You, Lord," I saw Jesus turn His face to the Father and smile! Thank You, Jesus, for the beautiful vision!

# Jesus Is Coming Soon!

The Lord Jesus Christ is in control of all things:
when the trumpet blows and when the choir sings.

Let everything that has breath worship Him.
Let everyone who has breath begin to sing.

Jesus is coming; He's coming for His Bride.
He's coming so soon: keep your ears and eyes opened wide.

There are earthquakes and wars and famines everywhere.
There are pestilences and droughts and bugs in the air.

So many signs of His soon-to-be return.
Please repent, be ready, don't be foolish and take the risk to forever burn.

Jesus is waiting at your heart's door, knocking and saying,
"Let Me come in, please," while many are praying.

"You must be born again to enter My kingdom,"
Jesus says in John 3:3.
Look in your Bible, look for yourself and you will see.

To be born again, believe on the Lord Jesus Christ—this is wise.
Repent of your sins, ask Him into your heart.
Here's where salvation lies.

When Jesus comes into your heart, you'll be changed forevermore.
You'll become like Him, you'll live in love and peace,
and you'll live eternally, for sure.

Today is the day of salvation— don't wait.
Say the sinner's prayer this moment,
and for sure you'll be walking through Heaven's Pearly Gates.

# *Day to Remember*

For there is born to you this day in the city of
David a Savior, who is Christ the Lord.
—Luke 2:1

On the day we call Christmas, a very long time ago,
a baby was born to a virgin. 'Tis so.

The baby, our Savior, was named Jesus Christ.
He was wrapped in swaddling clothes and laid in a manger, to be seen by many
    eyes.

A star shone from the Heavens and an angel declared,
"Your Savior is born! This Good News you must share!"

The wise men came from the Orient afar,
and traveled to see Him, being led by a star.

When they arrived at last, after a very long journey,
they gave Him their gifts and knew He would give them life eternally.

This baby's birth we celebrate each year,
and we praise the Heavenly Father for His gift to us so dear.

As we share the Good News of our Lord Jesus Christ,
His death on the Cross was done for all of us, a great sacrifice.

So accept the Lord Jesus, ask His forgiveness this hour.
Through His precious Blood is His saving power.

When you have been saved and He lives in your heart,
from His love, you'll never, ever want to depart.

He's the best Christmas gift you'll ever receive.
Be filled with His happiness and joy; don't let the devil cause you to be deceived.

Jesus loves you. He died for you. He'll fill you with His power.
Now go share Him with your friends. Don't wait; do it this very hour!

# Just Trust in Me

In my life, Lord, be glorified, be glorified:

The Lord said:

I am glorified in all of your prayers and all your praises to Me.
I hear your praises and look at your heart
and just see love for your Lord that you can't even see.

You are so constantly concerned with doing right before your Lord.
This is wisdom, you know.
To do otherwise you just can't afford.

It's just something that you have to trust in.
The Blood of Your Savior, He shed it for your sins.
Without faith in the Blood of Jesus, no one ever wins.

So try to rest, My daughter, Jesus paid the price, you see.
It's through His precious Blood He shed
that you already have the victory!

You have gone through so many trials that your Lord has brought you through,
and now you're going to have to trust in your Savior,
who has never, ever left you!

He has done a work in you that people will never know,
but when you get to Heaven,
your Lord will tell them and they'll praise Him so!

Now rest in Me, My daughter, for every need you have.
To bless you is My heart's desire; for you to worry makes Me sad.

*Prophetic Poetry*

You're the daughter of the Most High God,
joint heirs with the Lord Jesus Christ.
He died for you, He shed His Blood, so you could have eternal life!"

# Let My Light So Shine

Let my light so shine, Lord, let it shine bright
for Your Glory, Lord, both day and at night.

Let my light so shine, Lord, before all men
that they'll want what I have and be saved from their sins.

Let my light so shine, Lord, as it never has before.
Let Your Glory Cloud come down, Lord, and the latter rains begin to pour.

Let my light so shine, Lord, as my heart so desires.
Let the Holy Ghost anoint me and for You, Lord Jesus, set me on fire.

Let my light so shine, Lord, so that when I stand before men,
they'll not only hear Your Word, but Your Holy Ghost conviction,
will come down on them.

Let my light so shine before men, Lord, that they'll want to fall upon their knees,
and they'll cry out to You, Lord Jesus, save me, Jesus, save me, save me please!

# Letting Those Teens Know about Jesus

Thank you, Father for saving my soul.
Thank you, Lord Jesus, for making me whole.

Thank you, Lord Jesus, for keeping me in your care.
Thank you, Lord Jesus, for always being there.

I love you, Lord Jesus, with all of my heart.
I'd like that joy back, Jesus, that I had at the very start.

Please help me, Jesus, to know what it means
when I don't get to witness to all those young teens.

Help me, Lord Jesus, to just pray for them.
There are so many, I can only do what I can.

I just try so hard, Lord Jesus, to please You with all my heart,
I don't want to see those young teenagers not know You before they depart!

# *Linda*

My little girl Linda, whom I love so dear,
trust and obey Me and there will be no reason to fear.

I love you so much and I hear all your cries.
I see all those tears and I want to wipe your eyes.

Your heartaches have been so many,
that no one knows but your Lord,

but your heartaches will be over soon,
of that you can be sure.

Just remember, My child, that you are never ever alone.
It won't be long until you will finally be coming home.

Many, many things are going on in your life:
so much confusion, heartaches, and strife.

Just remember what My Word says:
that if you'll seek your Lord, who loves you, first,
the rest shall be added unto you, as you have read verse by verse.

In I Peter 2:24: "By My stripes you were healed."
I want you to allow Me to touch you and your needs will be filled.

You have so much loneliness, afraid to reach out.
So much rejection and abuse … of yourself, you have so much doubt.

Your sins, they've been forgiven.
Put them under the Blood and allow yourself to go on living.

*Prophetic Poetry*

All of My children have sinned and come short of the Glory of God.
Now go back to church, ask the Lord for His forgiveness, He loves you,
He is your Father God.

You have so many people there who want to love you so,
but you keep your hands out in front of you, saying, no, no, no!

Trust in me, My daughter, I live in all of them.
They want to love you, not hurt you. They'll help you to heal from within.

I know this is coming to you from your mother,
but trust me, she loves you so much, I could use no other!

Linda, come back to Me, I love you!
Jesus

# Look Who I've Found

"This is the day that the Lord has made; We shall rejoice and be glad in it." Psalm 119:2 (NKJV)

When He whispers to me, I love you, My child,
I want to tell others that about them He's just wild!

I push back the thoughts of where I was one day,
and where He has brought me is just too wonderful to say!

Where I once had such bitterness and anger and was so ill,
I now have such hope and happiness, I look forward to the day I no longer have to
    take a pill!

One by one He's taking them away.
Day by day He's healing me to do His will and to go His way!

He's my Savior, my master, my Lord and my King.
He's my teacher, my healer, my deliverer, my everything!

You see, since He saved me and I became His child,
He's made me that new Creation in Christ, so mild.

He's molded me and changed me as I've yielded to Him.
He's been so loving and patient, I'm just so in love with Him!

Jesus, my Savior, He's just so good to me!
As I look into His smiling face, His beautiful eyes are all I see.

He's the most beautiful person I've ever met in my life!
I love Him so much, He's taken away all my heartache and strife.

*Prophetic Poetry*

Being in His presence makes me want to praise Him and sing,
but I just sit very quietly and listen carefully to Him!

You see, He's saved me and loves me and I know I'm Heaven bound.
I just want to share Jesus with all: "Here He is, Our Savior, look who I've found!"

# Love

In my life, Lord, be glorified:

The Lord said:

And yes, I am glorified, as you listen to My voice.
To see you get up in the morning and see you sing and dance makes My heart
     rejoice.

You are My little girl who has gone through so many heartaches and so much pain.
But you just have to keep praising Me and loving Me. To do less, there is no gain.

You have so many gifts and talents that I want you to share.
To see you just give up on your life would be more than I could bear.

I have called you into the ministry of helping those in pain,
whether it be someone who is sick, or someone who has sinned and lives in
     constant shame.

Love is your first gift, the greatest of them all.
To reach out to hurting people and to love them is your call.

When I place you in a place of darkness, as My light you'll shine so bright.
Remember who you are in Me, a child of God. In you I live and together, there is
     great might.

So love those hurting people and show them that you're Mine.
Talk only of the good things and let your light so shine.

I'll speak through you so many times, they'll not know what to say.
And you'll have to just have trust in Me, that from Me you'll never stray.

You're just a willing vessel, a pilgrim on this earth.
As you share the love of Jesus, some will know the second birth.

Born Again is what to say, the Bible tells you so.
Just look at John 3:3; tell them it's in the Bible and they will know.

They'll come to you with questions and you'll help them understand
to be born again through your Lord Jesus is God's perfect plan.

# More Than a Conqueror

In the Name of Jesus, I am healed.
In the Name of Jesus, I am filled.
In the Name of Jesus, I belong to the Lord Jesus Christ.
He's the King of Kings, Lord of Lords, Almighty God.

In the name of Jesus, I am His and I am going to rise above.
When all those struggles, toils and strife come my way,
I will look to my Lord Jesus, lift up my hands and begin to pray.

So many times the devil says, you're defeated, you're too old, you just can't win.
But my Lord Jesus says in His Word, I'm more than a conqueror.
He shed His Blood and washed away all my sins.

The devil's a liar and walks around seeking whom he may devour.
But in my life, no more devil, I'll not give you another hour.

He can try to place his negative thoughts and speak his negative lies,
but no more will I receive them; through my Lord Jesus Christ, I'm too wise!"

So take that, devil, you thought you'd won again!
But through my Savior, the Lord Jesus Christ, I'm always going to win!

I'm a child of the Most High God.
I've been born of His Spirit and washed in His precious Son's Blood!

I'm going forth for the Lord Jesus Christ!
I'm a soldier of the Lord's, I've given Him my life!

As I go forth to be a servant of the Most High King,
I intend to praise the Lord, clap my hands, lift my head, and to Him, I will sing!

I've been given a gift and I praise my Lord.
The gift I've been given is called the gift of joy.

Promises of God are not to be taken lightly.
Just read His Word, believe what He says, and He'll bless us mightily!

# My Heart's Desire

I love you so much, My child,
who has been so gentle, patient, kind, and mild.

I love you, My daughter, who longs to do My will.
I love you so much. It's your cup I'm beginning to fill.

I love you so much, I'm taking you to another place.
It's where you will see love, mercy, and My grace.

It's My place, where you will sit, listen, and observe.
There will be many who will want you to begin to get busy and serve.

You must be very careful—it's My will you must do.
It's not My will that you work at this time. It's My will to bless you.

I have been watching you, running to and fro.
If it's not working, it's your mother, clothes to fold, grandchildren—
Where do they want to go?

You've had the awesome burden of caring for yourself.
But the needs of others must be met first, your needs are put on the shelf.

It's time for My daughter to get on her own.
I have a new husband, new workplace, and a brand new home.

Don't be alarmed if many shake their heads and say no, no, no.
They just don't realize how long this person's been waiting.
It's My timing, you can't go slow.

I will heal you, I will strengthen you.
I will prepare you to go My way.
This man is the one, you will be at his side. You will do as I say.

A long time ago, in a time of prayer we were.
Your heart was so willing, you said, "Send me, Lord, send me wherever."

It's your season now, My appointed time.
You gave Me your will and life, now you're all Mine!

I will use you for My Glory, and your husband as well.
You'll do work for Me, and to them of Jesus you will tell!

# My Assignment

It was Sunday afternoon at the park one day.
I heard the still small voice of the Holy Spirit say,

"Trust Me, My child, you have come through the fire
with many souls saved and seeds planted, just as I desired.

"You, My child, surrendered and said, 'Father, I give you my will.
Send me wherever with your Holy Spirit I am filled.'"

I've been baptized in the Holy Spirit; evangelism is my gift.
There are many souls out there needing Jesus in their hearts.
Only You, Holy Spirit, can help me with this.

Jesus is the one they're looking for,
but they are looking and seeking in every direction
while He's knocking on their hearts' door.

Help me, My Jesus, to be in the right place at the right time.
Place me in the right work where these lost souls I will find.

Retail is the place I will go, I said one day.
And much to my surprise, in two months, I was placed in the middle of that way.

They were not prepared for someone like me!
Smiling, thinking, I knew this is where I would be!

They thought they had trained me on their computers for my job,
but downstairs at the registers, I couldn't handle the mob.

So off they sent me to the fitting room job,
much to their surprise and to mine, but not to my God!

To Juniors they sent me, not what they had planned,
but exactly where those young souls were waiting,
and there was Jesus, writing in the sand!

He filled me with love and compassion as I looked at each one.
Their sins, all different, He showed me one by one.

I looked at them and smiled, and loved them as only Jesus could.
As they told me their stories, I shared with them Jesus, as I knew I should.

Without the Holy Spirit in me, I was powerless.
There was so much warfare, it was a mess!

You see, the devil doesn't like it when you tread on his ground,
but the Blessed Holy Spirit in me
led me and directed me. He moved me all around.

When my work was finished and the warfare so bad,
my work in the fitting room just made me sad.

Pain is all I felt in my legs and my back,
so I cried out to Jesus, "Help me Jesus, help!"
With the prayers of a phone counselor, "Jesus plucked my feet out of the net!"
Psalm 25:15 (NKJV)

# My Jesus

I lift my hands to You, Lord,
in reverence and in praise.

I will worship and adore You, Lord,
through all of my days.

I asked the Lord Jesus to help me with these feelings of guilt.
Jesus said to me, "Remember, My child, this is why My Blood was spilled!"

I love You, my Lord Jesus, and I thank You for saving me.
It's through Your Precious Blood You shed that I have total victory!

Help me, Lord Jesus, to have peace and joy within
and to always remember that Your Precious Blood was shed to deliver me from sin.

The devil walks around bringing up my past to me,
but through You, my Lord Jesus, I have already been made free.

The doubts and fears that come my way are from the accusing one,
but all I have to even do is to remember what my Savior did: Jesus,
God's Only Begotten Son.

# My Walk with You, Lord

I love you, my Savior, with all of my heart.
I have loved you, my Savior, from the very start.

As my years of growth have come, Lord Jesus, in my walk with You,
I have found, my Lord Jesus, that Your love is ever so true.

I have gone through many battles and trials in the past,
but I have found in trusting You that they just can't last.

I'm learning each day as the years go by
that I just have to keep praising You, and not to ask why.

In all of those trials, Jesus, I've always been aware
that no matter what I was going through, You were always there.

In the very darkest hours when I just wanted to come home,
I'd cry out, "Dear Lord Jesus, please don't leave me alone!"

I've just learned to lean on Jesus instead of wanting to go home!

You see, I know now that my Lord Jesus has a plan for my life.
This is why I've been through so much heartache, pain, and strife.

The devil has hated me from the very start,
especially now, because I gave Jesus my heart!

I'm going on with my Jesus. There's a work for me to do.
The harvest is ripe, but the laborers are few!

I know that the Lord has chosen for me
to bring in the lost and set the captives free.

This is a longing in me that is burning in my heart.
The Lord gave me this vision from the very start.

He has confirmed this to me just recently,
when He allowed me to be slain in the spirit in order to set me free.

I had such a longing to go on with Him,
but I was bound with such guilt, He had to set me free from this sin.

He carried that guilt on the Cross for me.
Through His precious Blood, I have been made free.

The Lord knows my hunger to study His Word,
and I know that my prayers to excel are being heard.

Being wise in this world means nothing to me.
Being wise in my Jesus gives me victory!

# No Other Way

Jesus, I love You so, I love You so, I love You so!
With all my heart, with all my mind, with all my strength,
much more it could not grow.

I love You, Holy Spirit, Your presence is so gentle.
I listen to Your still small voice within my heart. I know it is not mental.

Living Waters within my belly is what my Master said.
It is the Holy Spirit within, and by Him that I am led.

The Lord Jesus Christ has said to me,
I have come, that you would be made free.

It is so beautiful to know that Jesus is so real.
He has come to live within my heart and by the Holy Spirit I have been so healed.

I want my Holy Jesus to have His way in my heart.
I asked the Holy Spirit, of His gifts, to me impart.

I have asked my Holy Jesus to heal me of all my scars.
He knows His plans for me, but I do not know where or how far.

I trust in my Holy Jesus with every fiber of my being.
Through His Precious Blood He shed for me,
He's made me truly free.

I'm learning of my blessed Savior's love in a very special way
through the anointing of the Holy Spirit as I sit and I pray.

When we are out in the world, fulfilling our Lord's plan,
the devil often attacks us through our family or friends or, sometimes, just a man.

But the Lord tells us to love one another,
and what greater way than that our enemies with love we smother.

It's not through us that we can love in this way.
It's only through our Lord Jesus Christ in us. He's changing us every single day.

He's molding and shaping us as we yield our will to Him.
He's making us those pure and holy vessels, because He's saved us from all sin.

We are so blessed to be His children, you know.
Just be obedient to Him, He'll guide us in which way we're to go.

He's so special to me, I just love Him so.
I look at myself and think where I was, and where I am now—there's just no other
way to go!

Jesus said, "I am the Way, the truth, and the life. No one comes to the Father,
except through Me." John 14:6 (NKJV)

# Now Is the Time to Pray

Now is the time to begin to pray.
Pray in the night and pray in the day.

America has chosen to turn its back on My Chosen Ones, Israel.
All who were her enemies in Old Testament Days always fell.

It is written in My Word, 'tis so,
"I will bless those who bless you, and I will curse him who curses you." Gen:12:3
   (NKJV)
This you all know.

It is time to pray, my children who love My Son.
Not just a few, but every single one.

The time is very short. The coming of your Lord is near.
It is not a time to procrastinate. It is a time to pray with reverence and fear.

My children who pray with great diligence and seek My face
will receive My blessings, My joy, My peace, and My grace.

Those who are too busy and procrastinate
will put it aside and say, "This can wait."

There is not time to take this lightly. America has made its decision
to turn her back on My chosen ones and so will experience great division.

The blessings of God has been on America since the beginning of its time.
Now the blessings of God will only be on those who are Mine.

Now, My children, get down on your knees and pray for your president.
Pray for your government and your clergy this day.
Pray for all creation to come My Way.

This has to be done day by day.
Just remember to pray, pray, pray!

# Oh, to be Like You, Jesus

Oh to be like You, Lord Jesus, is the greatest desire of my heart.
Please take over my life, Lord Jesus, Your Spirit to me please impart.

As I have become born again this day,
I want only Your will and to walk in Your way.

Because You're my Savior and Lord of my life,
I can have peace and joy, instead of worry and strife.

You died for my sins on the Cross that day
because you knew, that as the Son of God, You were the only way.

You allowed them to pierce Your hands and Your feet
while beating Your back with those stripes, knowing it was for me.

Had I been there, I would have cried and screamed,
but You would have said, " Quiet, My child, it's not like it seems.

"You see, My child, I have to die on this Cross this day.
It's for the sins of the world, a price I am willing to pay.

"A Sacrificial Lamb has been chosen—that's Me.
I'm Jesus Christ, the Messiah, I'm to die on a tree.

"I'll arise again in three days, this you will see,
and all who accept Me will be My children and from all sin be free.

"So come to Me, My children, time is so short.
Don't laugh and mock other Christians and think it's a sport.

"If you'll accept Me as your Savior, you'll be forgiven of all sins,
and live forever in Heaven with Me and your Heavenly Father.
　　　It's the only way to win."

Heaven is real, and Hell is too.
Jesus will save you, Satan will kill you!

Make a choice today, it's now or never.
For today may be the last day you will have to savor.

# Some Day

I worship You, Lord Jesus, the Lord of Lords and King of Kings.
I praise You, Lord Jesus, the creator of everything.

My Lord Jesus, You are worthy of all praise and glory.
What You've done in my life, I could write a story.

Every time I think of You, I praise You and I want to sing.
What You've done for all mankind
should cause them to praise You as their Lord and King.

Oh, my Savior, Lord and King,
You're my Master, healer, my everything.

You're worthy of such praise, my Lord.
To do less, I just cannot afford.

You are so full of love and mercy and yes, Your Grace!
I often pray, my beautiful Lord, just to see Your face.

Although I know this cannot yet be,
there will come a day when Your face I will see!

# Thank You, Jesus

In my life, Lord, be glorified:

The Lord said:

I am glorified.
I am glorified.
In your life, I have always been glorified.

I have saved your soul,
and I have made you whole.

You have been such a blessing to Me,
I have set your heart free.

You have been accused of many, many things,
but all you have done is praise Me and sing.

There are many, many people who are looking for a person
who has done everything they can to be holy, that's for certain.

About this person, they begin to talk.
When it comes to them, they can't walk the walk!

So when persecution comes your way, and it does nearly every day,
just say, Thank you, Jesus, for making my day!

*Prophetic Poetry*

So be prepared, it's coming soon.
Continue to read My Word, pray in the spirit,
and to My still small voice, you'll be in tune.

I need you out there; you have a sweet spirit that comes from Me,
and with you and Me together, they'll know Jesus and they too will have the victory!

# The Blizzard of 2003

It was a snowy night in the month of February.
I was so aware of our Holy God's caring.

It was a blizzard, they announced on the TV news, maybe two feet, they said.
I was just excited, but to many, there was great fear and dread!

There were so many running to and fro
getting needed supplies—you know how it goes.

Christians were resting, watching preachers on the TV.
Others were snowmobiling and shoveling, thinking they were free.

No school tomorrow, no work tomorrow, another day to rest.
But little do they realize, this could be the beginning of a really big test.

Were they ready to meet their Maker, as many men would say?
Not stopping to think that today is the day of salvation, they really need to pray!

There are wars and rumors of wars all over the world of which we have no power.
There are pestilences, starving children, people's hearts failing them from fear this
    very hour.

It's all in the Bible, read it for yourself.
People are sharing the Good News of the Lord Jesus Christ, of what it's all about.

But many are not ready, they don't want to hear it, not this day.
They don't have time, they don't believe it, many will say.

Just don't wait too long, your day might come now.
When you meet your Maker, the Lord Jesus Christ,
He'll just let you know, He's knocked at your heart's door so many times and you've
just kept Him out.

He'll tell you, "I did not know you," and He'll tell you with a shout!

Please receive Christ Jesus, read your Bible and pray.
He's coming soon to get His Church and He wants to come for you, to take you
away.

# The Glory of the Lord is Upon Me

I have been called to bring the Good News of the Lord Jesus to many.
I am to share His love and His peace to all who will receive it, if any.

Trusting the Lord and doing His will is all I long to do.
Sharing the Good News is not an easy task, but this I will always do.

I love the Lord Jesus with all of my heart and all of my soul and all of my strength.
To share what He's done for the whole world on the Cross, I will go to any length.

I would go into the jungles, I would go into the Ukraine,
I would go to the ends of the earth and never refrain.

It's the Lord's will I choose, not my own, 'tis true.
I hunger and I thirst for more of my Lord Jesus. I can't get enough,
    I can't get enough of You!

*Prophetic Poetry*

# The Only Way to Me

In my life, Lord, be glorified, be glorified:

And I am glorified, said The Lord.
As you sit at My feet, singing to Me so sweet,
at this very time, our hearts do meet.

You glorify Me by singing to Me.
You glorify Me, lifting your hands to Me.
You glorify Me, being obedient to Me.

It isn't easy being a child of God.
To fail Him, sometimes causes me sob!

As David was a man after My own Heart,
he never wanted from Me to depart.

His sins were many, of some he knew.
When he saw he'd done wrong, to Me he quickly drew.

"Forgive me, My Lord," he'd cry with great pain.
"Of what I've done before You, there is no gain.

"Your Spirit, oh Lord, don't take it away.
Please forgive me Lord," I'd hear him pray.

He knew of his sin and he hated it so.
But the devil had tempted him of Me to let go.

You see, the devil deceives, he tempts, and destroys.
But to Me, My children are not just little toys.

They're My children, they've been bought with a price.
The Blood of My Son Jesus Christ, He has paid the price!

So My Son, He is praying for My children always
to be strong and courageous and to walk in My ways.

He knows of your frailties and has compassion and wants you to win.
But you must be strong and courageous and not let the devil in.

You see, the devil is a defeated foe.
He lost when My Son Jesus said, "Father, forgive them, for they do not know."

Through the Blood of Jesus Christ is the only way to victory.
Through the Blood of My Son Jesus is the only way to Me!

# Unforgiveness

In my life, Lord, be glorified:

The Lord said:

You have glorified Me in your deeds every day.
You have a pure heart, your desire is to walk in My Way.

Each day you sit at My Feet and praise Me and worship Me and pray.
I am blessed, I am glorified and in your life, people will know that I am the Way.

You have much to do for your Lord, My Child.
You are the one who has chosen to allow Me to make you so sweet
    and kind and mild.

You're made in My image, My Child, so sweet.
As you seek My presence, our hearts do meet.

You will be used to help the hurting ones,
those wounded by words, with wounds inside,
wounds seen only by your Lord, your Savior and yes, I have cried.

You have been one of those with wounds so deep within,
but you have allowed Me to take you through the fire,
for you know unforgiveness was one of your sins.

You will pray for those with wounds so deep,
and you will teach those, like you, that unforgiveness, they cannot keep.

So trust Me, My Child, I love you so.
You have a calling on your life, and I will not let you go.

# Watch Our Words

In my heart, Lord, be glorified:

The Lord said:

Every day I am glorified in your heart, My child.
What I want is to be glorified through your life, My child, so very mild.

As you were a blessing to so many this day,
I saw the sweet fragrance of your Lord, much to the world's dismay.

You were so sweet and gentle with that elderly child of mine,
she just felt so amazed that you were so gentle, tender, and kind.

You see, she had been told so many things that were not true,
things that were unkind and she considered they were about you.

The devil roams around seeking whom he may devour.
He also tells many lies and also is a coward.

The Holy Ghost reveals the truth at the very perfect hour,
always much to their surprise, those who roam and seek to devour.

The devil uses people to do his dirty work.
The principalities and powers in the Heavens
will always find someone willing to dig up his dirt.

But much to their great surprise,
the Lord will always open their eyes.

What seemed to be all right to say
was not to God, much to their dismay.

Down on their knees they will go with a bang.
"Oh, God forgive me," and their heads they will hang.

I should not have said that, it wasn't true!
What I said about them, I was saying about You.

Oh Lord, please search my heart and show me my wicked ways,
and the Lord will say, "You are forgiven, just lift your hands to Me in praise."

So you see, My child, each one is guilty of saying things they should not
and doing things that are sin to your Lord, but they have been forgotten.

Because your Savior, the Lord Jesus Christ, shed His Blood for you,
just repent, begin to pray, that's all you have to do.

# The Way

In my life, Lord, be glorified:

I love You, Lord, with all of my heart,
    I often wish I could depart.

But I'm not here to serve myself,
    I'm here to help others, to know the love of God as I have felt.

I'm just a pilgrim on a short journey,
    working for the Lord, here on earth and then on to Heaven for the rest of
    eternity.

The burdens get heavy and the trials and tribulations too,
    but when I sit at the feet of my Savior in worship,
    He reminds me, saying, "My child, I love you."

He holds my hand wherever I may be.
    His presence I'm aware of, His face I cannot see.

It's in my mind I must remember I'm never ever alone.
    I'm not ever without my Savior, but often look forward to my
    going Home.

I've been called to suffer, as my Savior did.
    He was mocked and laughed at and so much more, but He never, ever hid.

He knew He'd been sent here for one purpose only,
    to shed His Blood on the Cross for the sins of mankind,
    but at times He found Himself to be very lonely.

As I have been called aside to become one with Him,
   loneliness, rejection, and sadness I often feel within.

But I'm more than a conqueror through my Lord Jesus Christ and destined to
   win.
I'll run the race, not looking back, knowing always He's at my side,
   and I've been redeemed from all my sins.

I'm looking forward to being with Him,
   so I must keep pressing on in order to win.

"Well done, my good and faithful servant," I'll hear Him say.
   "It's through your obedience that you've come My way.

"Now get up and get ready for another day,
   and help Me to help you to show them the Way.

# There's Nothing I'd Rather Do

There's nothing so sweet
as to sit at Your feet.
There's nothing that I'd rather do
than to be like You.

There's nothing out there
that makes me want to care
about the things of the world—this is true.

There's troubles and woes,
there's friends and there's foes.
Who to trust is a guess,
only God knows best.

So we take our cares to Him,
asking forgiveness of our sins,
trusting He'll deliver us
from anything.

Asking daily, "Give me wisdom in all that I do,
pleasing You, in doing Your will, is all I really want to do."

Please, Lord, give me strength, give me power
to get through my every hour.

Praising You and thanking You is how I fight the battle through,
trusting in Your Holy Word, knowing every word is true!

You are my Master and my King.
You are my Lord, my everything.
You are the creator of all things.

# They Too Will Have the Victory

I love you, My child, so pure and so sweet.
I love you, My child, as you sit at My feet.

As you sing your praises and worship Me so,
I can see in your heart, "Lord, don't let me go!"

You try so very hard to please every person you see,
when all you really have to do is care about pleasing Me.

I am your God, there is no man above Me.
By keeping your focus on your Savior, that's when you'll have the victory.

Don't ever think your children aren't in My perfect plan.
They have a calling on their lives and they'll always serve Me, not man.

There are many religious spirits in the church you're going to,
but there are religious spirits in every church, 'tis true.

So be prepared, the Rapture could be soon.
Continue to read My Word and to My still small voice be in tune.

I need you out there, you have a sweet spirit that comes from Me.
Together they'll know Jesus, and they too will have the victory!

# To Be His Child

When I was a brand new creature in Christ Jesus, to be His child was so exciting!
I just wanted my friends to open their hearts and also welcome Him in!

Everyone looked at me as though I had lost my mind,
but to have the Lord Jesus Christ as your Savior,
there isn't anything greater to find.

So many people are so busy trying to find love and peace and riches.
When you find the Lord Jesus as your Savior, you're happy if you're digging ditches.

He'll give you all the riches in your life you'll ever desire.
Just answer His call on your life and He'll fill you with the Holy Ghost and Fire.

You see, Jesus has a plan for your life, just give your will to Him.
You will have all those riches, peace and joy—they will come from deep within.

You see, we have an enemy who is out to rob, steal, and destroy,
but having the Lord Jesus as our Savior,
we are His children, not just a toy.

# Trust Me, My Child

Trust Me, My child, in all that you do.
Trust Me, My child; I will always come through.

Trust Me always, no matter what the situation is.
Thank Me and praise Me through all that's going on
and you will always see My Hand at work. That's just the way it is!

Always remember that you are My child.
You are mild and meek, not rebellious and wild.

The devil may try to destroy you and rob you of your joy,
but through the Lord Jesus, My Son, the devil will find that you're not a toy.

You're My child, made in My image,
a joint heir with Jesus, and your work isn't finished.

You're going to come through with such a victory,
a great testimony to share, giving all the glory to Me!

You've already gone through more than most could comprehend,
but remember: It's almost over. It's coming to an end.

Very soon, My Church will hear the trumpet blow and My children
    shall arise.
"Come home quickly," the Lord Jesus will cry!

*Prophetic Poetry*

"Come home, My children, I have rest for you!
There will be peace, joy, and no more tears, 'tis true."

Keep your eyes on Jesus through everything.
Remember He loves you, just sing and sing and sing!

# When Jesus Died on the Cross

Suddenly there came a great darkness upon the earth.
There were earthquakes, people running, children screaming. They hadn't known
of this Man's birth.

"What have we done? What have we done? We were told that we could choose.
We did not know we put on the Cross the real King of the Jews!"

As the earth trembled from the Father's grieving heart,
He remembered the words of His dying Son, "Father, I give you my spirit," as from
this earth He did depart.

"He had to be the Messiah," one man was heard to say.
"We have done a terrible thing! We have sinned against God on this very day!"

As His spirit departed from Jesus' body and went to Hell for us,
He fought the devil, demons alike, was resurrected, now seated beside the Father,
interceding for each of us.

The devil caused the people to crucify our Lord, thinking he had won.
But oh how wrong he was—this was God's Only Begotten Son!

Jesus is the living God; He's coming back real soon!
So be alert, read the Word, to the Spirit of the Lord, be in tune.

Go in peace to all the lost, sharing with them the Good News
that Jesus lives, He died for their sins. "Tell them," He says, "It is I that you must
choose!"

"Tell them, 'You must repent of your sins this very day! . . .
Let Jesus become your Savior. Ask Him into your heart. It's the only way!'"

Heaven is real; it's where Jesus is waiting for you.
There are peace, joy, golden streets, and mansions; this is all true.

But then there's also Hell, a place of deep despair.
There's wailing, gnashing of teeth, and darkness; you'll burn forever in torment if
    you are there.

Please make your choice, and please make it today.
Jesus died for your sins. He loves you. He is the only way!

# The Salvation Prayer

All men are lost apart from the saving grace of Jesus Christ and sin is cleansed and salvation is received only through repentance and faith in the Atoning Blood of Jesus Christ.

And he brought them out and said, "Sirs, what must I do to be saved?" So they said, "Believe on the Lord Jesus Christ, and you will be saved, you and your household." Acts 16:30-31 (NKJV)

" … if you confess with your mouth the Lord Jesus and believe in your heart that God has raised Him from the dead, you will be saved. For with the heart one believes unto righteousness, and with the mouth confession is made unto salvation." Romans 10:9-10 (NKJV)

"For all have sinned, and come short of the glory of God." Romans 3:23 (KJV)

If you have not repented of your sins and asked the Lord Jesus Christ to be the Lord of your life, just pray this prayer:

Dear Heavenly Father, I come to you in the Name of the Lord Jesus Christ, confessing that I am a sinner. Please forgive me of my sins. I do believe in Your Son, the Lord Jesus Christ and what He did for me on the Cross at Calvary. I thank you Lord Jesus for your precious blood that You shed for my sins and for the stripes You received on Your back for my healings. I believe that You died on the Cross at Calvary and on the third day, You were resurrected from the dead and are now seated at the right hand of God the Father Almighty. Lord Jesus, please come into my heart and be the Lord of my life. Amen.

*Prophetic Poetry*

What to do now:

Find a good, Bible-teaching church and a good study Bible. Attend church each Sunday, and get into a Bible study with other believers. You will not only learn from the Bible, but you will get to make new friends who also are believers of Jesus. Begin praying and talking to the Lord on a daily basis.

# Patricia Johnson

was born and raised most of her life in the Middletown, Delaware area. She graduated in 1958, was saved in 1980, and had been married for twenty-seven years. One night her husband told her it was him or God! This meant a divorce! She tried marriage a second time, but soon found she had made an unwise decision. It just wasn't a good thing! One day after her devotions, she heard the Holy Spirit say, "What's more important, material things or her health?" She knew she had to leave, and quickly! She has lived with her son, Chris Buckworth and his family for 15 years now, and she has a daughter, Linda Barrett, and 5 grandsons, ages nineteen to thirty-two. She also has a great-grandson, 5yrs. of age. She now lives her life for the Lord Jesus and feels so blessed to have such a wonderful family, who also serve the Lord!